Why does Art Therapy work?

Why does Art Therapy work?

Written by

Dr. Austin Mardon

Catherine Mardon

Haya Sonawala

Anna Yang

Seonmin Jeong

Khushi Shah

Terrence Wu

Ashmita Mazumder

Edited by

Kathryn Carson

Taryn Foster

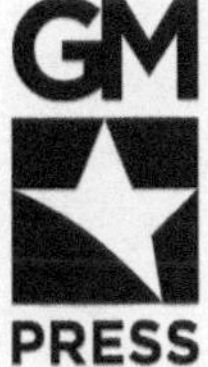

First Printing: 2021

Cover Design and typeset by Clare Dalton

ISBN 978-1-77369-624-9

E-book ISBN 978-1-77369-625-6

Golden Meteorite Press

103 11919 82 St NW

Edmonton, AB T5B 2W3

www.goldenmeteoritepress.com

CONTENTS

Chapter 1:

The history
of
art therapy

Written by Haya Sonawala

Today's world is permeated with the narrative that one must be productive at all times. This may be why a career in the arts is often overlooked—as it is difficult to make money unless the artist is creating to appease others. However, it is not the case that there is no value in art. In a world that focuses on the value the creative process can generate, perhaps engaging with art for the sake of the art is part of what can make it so therapeutic; it is a break from the norms of everyday life. Most people go into therapy for one of two reasons—tightening or loosening. Those who need tightening are looking to ground themselves and reconnect with their surroundings. Those who need loosening, on the other hand, are looking to let go of the expectations and pressures placed on them and learn how to engage meaningfully with their lives and the world around them. The latter is much more common.[1] This is where art becomes important—it helps people communicate in nonverbal ways, better understand themselves and their experiences, as well as provides them with an escape from their everyday life. In doing this, it provides them with a safe space to explore and understand a world that they may otherwise view as inaccessible.

Art Before Art Therapy

Art, of course, existed before art therapy, and it continues to exist without the formal word "therapy". Yet, even without that, the arts have always been known as a form of self expression. Pablo Picasso claimed that "art washes away from the soul the dust of everyday life".[2] The arts have long been, and continue to be, a form of expression that can offer catharsis, inner peace, and self reflection. In doing so, they can act as an aid to mental health, regardless of whether it is experienced on one's own or with the guidance of a therapist.

Taoism and Art Before Art Therapy

Many ancient cultures have used the arts for cleansing, expression, and inner peace, and these uses can be found in the practices of Taoism. Today, expressive arts therapy is centred around the concept of poiesis, which traditionally is "a productive activity guided by the consciousness and will of the artist".3 In the context of expressive arts therapy however, both the therapist and the patient must "let go of knowing and willing".3 This is further enforced by Abraham Maslow, who wrote about this Taoist philosophy. He "recommended a nonactive, noninterfering contemplation of a client's problem, rather than analytical, premature intervention".4 This concept runs parallel to the concept of wu-wei in Taoism, which is the concept of non-action, or attention to process.3 This idea places importance on the other-worldness of the imagination and "takes the client and therapist into a realm of non-ordinary reality in which resources can be developed and new possibilities for action discovered".3 The practices and philosophies that are now common in present day art therapy has many roots in many different cultures.

The Role of the Artist

The practice of art therapy began in the 1940s, but the study of art was prevalent well before that, and artists needed a way to earn a living. Before the prevalence of art therapy, career options for art students were limited. They could become art teachers, or become commercial artists, but both had drawbacks. Teaching positions were insufficient, and most artists wanted to have the time to focus on their own work, which teaching full time did not allow them to do. Commercial artists felt that they were not working creatively, and they "did not think of themselves as creative artists but rather as craftsmen"[5] who are creating work for others rather than creating work that they want to create, echoing Oscar Wilde's opinion that "[t]he moment that an artist takes notice

of what other people want, and tries to supply the demand, he ceases
to be an artist, and becomes a dull or an amusing craftsman, an honest
or dishonest tradesman".[6] This distinction, the distinction between an
artist and a tradesman, highlights the importance of creative freedom to
an artist, because an art student presumably hopes to be creative, and
having to step into the role of a tradesman would be disappointing and
distressing. As a result, favourable opportunities for arts students before
the 1940s were scarce, which discouraged the study and practice of art,
and further enforced academic art, or high art, in that only the wealthy
were able to pursue the arts.[5]

Art Therapy and Child Art

Art therapy can be said to have found its roots in art education, as
many of the founders of art therapy were first involved in the field.
Historically, art has been an area of study for those in society that are
incredibly privileged. It was reserved for the upper class and nobility
until the late 19th century, when child art became popularized under
the Secession movement,[5] which was formed in 1897.[7] This movement
aimed to "break with previous classical art movements, to make a
critical assault on the bourgeoisie, and to seek refuge from the pressures
of the external world".[5] Fundamental to this movement was the "belief
that the arts could promote change and liven up a jaded culture, in the
case of post-Empire and post-war depression".[5] This movement presents
one example in which it is hoped that art will have a positive impact on
mental health and morale.

This term "child art", which was popularized around this time, was
coined by Franz Cizek, an Austrian painter who was associated with
the Secession movement. He was "one of Austria's most progressive
art teachers" in that he rejected traditional methods of teaching art,
and instead believed that all children "had the potential for creative
expression", and all of his students were encouraged by him to engage
in that expression.[5]

This idea of free expression is now commonplace in art therapy, but at the time it was just a progressive view of visual art, one that strayed from the traditional academic art that was prevalent at the time. Child art was once considered crude,[5] yet in today's context of art therapy that would not matter, because it is "more about the process than the quality of the end product".[8] This idea is seen in Cizek's methods, in that he "believed the teacher's function was to create an atmosphere conducive to creative work, to gain rapport with the children and take them seriously, and to provide love, security, and significance".[5]

Cizek went as far as to request permission from the Vienna school board for a new school that aimed "to let children grow, develop and mature".[5] Although this request was first denied, Cizek received permission in 1897 to open an art class which became so successful "he was offered rooms in the state art school".[5] In this way, Cizek was able to further spread his progressive opinions and practices regarding art. These ideas grew in popularity beyond Vienna by one of his biographers and disciples, Wilhelm Viola, who brought his ideas to Britain.[5]

According to psychoanalyst David Winnicott, creative impulses and expressions were a prerequisite to human development. An early example of this can be seen in infants and their relationship to transitional objects, those that are of extreme importance to the child and the loss of which can cause extreme distress. These objects essentially form a bridge between the baby and the outside world, and the baby learns to manipulate these objects in creative manners to meet their needs or to amuse themselves. These behaviours are thought to then lead to creative responses such as drawing and painting. The ability to be creative was often linked with psychological health. These discoveries lead to Winnicott's work finding a prominent place in art therapy and its foundation, despite him not having written about art therapy itself.[5]

Art therapy practices today strongly echo Cizek's opinions about art-teaching. His philosophy has "a clear parallel with the basic principles of non-directive art therapy", in which the therapist provides space and materials, doing so in a non-judgemental way, simply allowing the patients to develop themselves through their creative work.[5] Art therapy promotes self-expression, independence, problem-solving skills, and develops interpersonal skills, communication, and empathy.[9] This is true of adult and child patients alike. These parallels suggest the importance of Cizek's progressive views and practices in the development of art therapy, and the idea that visual art can help promote personal development as well as treat mental health issues.

The Beginnings: Art Therapy in the 1940s

*Art and Mental Health in the 1940s*At the time, psychiatry was not "generally viewed as a prestigious area of medicine and mental health has not been well funded".[5] Those who did suffer with mental health issues were regarded with fear and misunderstanding by the general public. Research in the area was also limited, which only furthered ignorance amongst the population.[5]

The term "Art Therapy" itself was coined by artist Adrian Hill,[5] when he himself had to spend some time in a hospital when he contracted tuberculosis. His treatment required a large amount of rest in a quiet environment. However, Hill took a dislike to the lack of visual stimulation in the hospital. In order to pass the time, he began to draw. In doing so, "he found that the problem of how to occupy his mind and emotions … had been largely solved as he quickly became involved in his own art work again".[5] Although he did not think to share this with other patients during his time in the hospital, Hill later worked with a department of occupational therapy as an art teacher to help patients pass their time while doing an activity that was "designed to distract traumatised minds from distressing thoughts".[5] However, in contrast to Cizek's beliefs regarding art teaching, Hill was critical of the patients' work. Upon furthering his work, he discovered that becoming acquainted with each patient's medical history would help him direct them towards more individualized treatment.

Adrian Hill and Marie Petrie, who wrote with the content of the national regeneration movement that followed World War II, "believed that art might have the power to restore lost health, but this could only be a certain kind of art".[5] They believed that art created order amidst an increasingly chaotic world. The practice of art therapy first began being widely and formally used in health settings after the Second World War.[8] Many soldiers and civilians were healing from not only the war, but from the compounded effects of living through two great wars during their lifetimes. Many experienced difficulties in readapting to a peacetime lifestyle, which created a need for new approaches to treating mental illness. It became particularly useful in treating post traumatic stress disorder. Recent studies that focused on using art therapy and group therapy—both of which became prevalent in the aftermath of the Second World War—found that these forms of therapy lead to an increase in humour, self esteem, and creative problem-solving.[10]

The Role of the Artist

As previously stated, the career outlook for art students was unfavourable; most had to choose between teaching and being a commercial artist, both of which had many drawbacks. Career choice forced them to choose between the streams of art appreciation and art creation.

The rise of art therapy offered art students and artists a third and more favourable career option. With the advent of the field, students had a career prospect that not only had an abundance of openings, but also one that paid similar to that of the role of a commercial artist and offered similar working conditions, as well as gave them enough time to focus on their own work. It also "would seem to satisfy a need to use art skills in an obviously socially useful way, while at the same time giving scope to preserving an identity as an artist".[5]

Art therapy has come a long way since its conception in the 1940s, and from its roots well before that. Now, art therapy is a common and popular form of therapy that is accessible to all people. It is not limited to artists, the way art itself was at one point in time, nor is it limited to children, the way it was when Cizek was first exploring the processes and philosophies that eventually lead to contemporary art therapy practices. As well, it is not as critical as it was under the instruction of Adrian Hill. Now, art therapy provides an open and non-judgemental space for anyone struggling with their mental health.

Chapter 2:

What is art therapy?

Written by Anna Yang

Introduction

People have been relying on the arts as a means of communication, self-expression, and healing for thousands of years.[1] This ancient link forms the premise for art therapy, but even so, art therapy didn't become a formal practice until the 1940s, when doctors began to note that individuals living with mental illness often expressed themselves through drawings and other artworks.[1] This observation led many to explore the use of art as a healing strategy, and since then art has become a key component of the therapeutic field.[1] The rise of art therapy was precipitated in large part by Margaret Naumburg, often known as the "mother of art therapy."[2] Naumburg was influenced by the first wave of psychoanalytic theory in the early 20th century and believed that the creative process could allow individuals to bring to light unconscious thought and feelings they might have repressed.[2] She felt that talking through this creative process with a therapist could help individuals understand what their artwork could reveal to them about themselves, and this understanding would, in turn, promote psychological healing.[2] Her writings continue to be influential in the 21st century, as art therapy has grown in popularity.[2] This chapter will provide an overview of what art therapy is, some of its uses, as well as what a typical art therapy session looks like.

What is Art Therapy

Art therapy is the use of artistic methods to treat psychological disorders and/or enhance mental health.[1] It is a form of expressive therapy which is rooted in the idea that the creative process of making art can foster healing and improve one's physical, mental, and emotional well-being.[3] Art therapy facilitates this healing by combining psychotherapy with the creative process — using imagery, colour, and shape as part of a creative therapeutic approach helps clients express thoughts and feelings that are otherwise difficult to articulate.[4] Art therapy engages all of the senses in order to relax the nervous system and improve self-regulation, reduce anxiety, improve executive functioning, and help the client feel more in control.[4] There is a wealth of literature that supports the efficacy of art therapy, although some findings are mixed.[1] Studies on art therapy are often small and inconclusive, so further research is still needed to more closely examine when art therapy is most beneficial and how to make it as effective as possible.[1]

Art therapy sessions are administered by art therapists, who are professionals trained in both art and therapy.[3] They tend to be knowledgeable about matters such as human development, psychological theories, clinical practice, the healing potential of art, spiritual, multicultural, and artistic traditions, and are experienced in using this knowledge to facilitate clients' healing through creative processes.[3] Through the use of art-making, discussions and reflections on the artwork, and relationship building, art therapists are able to support clients in problem-solving, developing self-awareness, improving self-esteem, managing stress, and enhancing interpersonal skills to achieve mental wellness.

A wide variety of artistic techniques can be used in art therapy, including drawing, painting, colouring, doodling, collage, finger painting, photography, sculpting, and pottery.[1] As clients create art using any of these techniques, they are engaging in a creative process that helps them resolve the issues they are facing, develop and manage their feelings and behaviours, reduce stress, and improve their self-awareness and self-esteem.[3] As clients create their artwork, as well as afterward, they may analyze what they have made and how it makes them feel. Through these acts of exploration, clients can identify themes and conflicts that are affecting their thoughts, emotions, and behaviours.[1] People who make art in any form are taking part in a process of self-discovery that gives them a safe space to express their feelings and allows them to feel more in control of their lives.[2] It is this therapeutic potential of art-making that art therapy seeks to use to improve people's well-being.

Uses of Art Therapy

Art therapy is incredibly versatile; art therapists work with individuals, couples, families, and groups from diverse backgrounds and in a wide variety of settings including but not limited to inpatient care, outpatient clinics, long term care homes, rehabilitation units, mental health agencies, schools, and correctional institutes.[4] Art therapy has proven to be beneficial in the treatment of a wide range of mental disorders and forms of psychological distress, with research studies demonstrating its efficacy in areas such as substance use disorders, developmental disabilities, coping with physical health conditions such as cancer, struggles with mental illnesses such as depression and anxiety, grief, trauma and post-traumatic stress disorder, and issues related to aging.[4] In many cases, art therapy is used in conjunction with other psychotherapy techniques such as cognitive behavioural therapy and group therapy.[1] In this section, a few common uses of art therapy will be discussed in greater detail.

Trauma

In studies of adults who have experienced trauma, art therapy has been found to significantly reduce trauma symptoms and levels of depression.[4] A possible explanation for this is as follows. Research has shown that trauma is stored in the brain as a sensory experience, consisting primarily of fragments of images and sensations as opposed to a coherent cognitive narrative.[4] To compensate for this, a sensory experience such as art therapy can provide a vehicle for the externalization of traumatic experiences and the subsequent release of tension.[4] Additionally, the kinesthetic experience of art-making may serve to enhance a relaxation response and increase one's ability to tolerate future stressors.[4] The resulting artwork can serve as a symbol and container of the effects of the client's trauma, helping them integrate the experience and associated feelings into their life narrative.[4] The steps that follow this process of art-making, such as the manipulation of the product and the guided discussion with the art therapist, may further help the client learn to modulate their emotions and strengthen their sense of control.[4]

Children

Art therapy for children typically emphasizes confidentiality, independence, and self-regulation, all of which are important in any art therapy session but are particularly crucial when the client is a youth.[4] Common uses of art therapy for young clients include helping with behavioural issues, depression, anxiety and stress, attention deficit disorder/attention deficit hyperactivity disorder, autism spectrum disorder, learning disabilities, developmental disabilities, anger management, grief and loss, bullying or social isolation, trauma, attachment difficulties, and identity exploration.[4] Art therapy can be particularly beneficial for children by providing them with psychosocial support, increasing relaxation and reducing anxiety and agitation, helping build interpersonal skills, increasing meaningful and positive interactions with family and friends, increasing self-awareness, building positive coping mechanisms, and promoting freedom of choice, a sense of achievement, and a sense of mastery. All of these skills and qualities can increase a youth's self-esteem during a critical phase of mental and emotional development.[4]

Seniors

Techniques that are commonly used in art therapy with seniors include painting and drawing, collage, photography, sewing and weaving, pottery, woodworking, and creative writing.[4] Art therapy can help seniors cope with major physical, psychological, and life changes, grief and loss, depression, anxiety, loneliness, sensory-motor difficulties, cognitive decline, addiction, trauma, and unresolved conflicts.[4] The opportunity to be creative and make their own choices during an art therapy session can help seniors rekindle new energy, and the process of art-making can also assist seniors by stimulating the senses and sharpening perceptual and cognitive skills.[4] The social interactions that clients have with their art therapists and the opportunity to gain recognition for their artistic accomplishments can also help reduce feelings of isolation and loneliness, which are common obstacles faced by seniors.[4] Additionally, the final outcome of creating a tangible art product can help seniors maintain a sense of pride and dignity, both of which are crucial to the preservation of a high level of self-esteem.[4] These links between art therapy for seniors and improved health outcomes are supported by research. For instance, one study found that art therapy reduced depression and increased self-esteem in older adults living in nursing homes.[1]

What an Art Therapy Session Looks Like

There is a degree of flexibility to every therapy session, yet even so, art therapy stands out as one of the most flexible forms of therapy both in terms of establishing a plan for treatment and in terms of what each therapy session might look like. Every art therapist has their own unique approach, and the approach chosen for each client is likely to vary according to their needs and goals. For instance, the approach one uses with a client striving for recovery from trauma is likely to differ greatly from the approach one uses with a child struggling with identity issues. The multitude of different art activities that can be used in any particular session further compounds the number of different trajectories an art therapy session could potentially follow, and as such, it is incredibly difficult to call any particular art therapy session "typical." This being said, art therapists do often have schedules to adhere to, which often leads to the development of more structured therapy sessions. In particular, art therapy that is delivered in structured environments such as schools, hospitals, and prisons often have a greater emphasis on outcomes with a direct request for proof that an art therapy program is working and producing desirable results.[5] Art therapists working in these settings may adopt more structured therapy session plans to ensure that the desired outcomes are being attained in the required timeframe.[5] More broadly speaking, some structure is helpful in any art therapy session to ensure that both the therapist and client remain focused on the issues that the client seeks to resolve.

In general, an art therapy session has three stages: pre-art making, art making, and post-art making.[5] The first stage, pre-art making, consists primarily of assessing the client, as well as providing preliminary information that the client needs to know before the art therapy session begins in earnest.[5] If the session in question is the client's first, it will likely involve a detailed process where the art therapist collects information about the client and the precipitating factors that led them to make the therapy appointment.[5] The therapist may also choose to take the opportunity to educate the client regarding the concept of art therapy by outlining its benefits, discussing what sessions will generally look like, and addressing any doubts that the client might have regarding participating in art activities, therapy, or both.[5] A common reassurance that the therapist will give the client at this point is that there is no right or wrong way to make art in an art therapy session — the art need not be pretty or precise.[6] On the other hand, if the client is a returning client, the the pre-art making stage is likely to be much shorter, perhaps merely involving a brief discussion of how the client is currently feeling, as well as any issues that have arisen since the last therapy session.[5] Another key part of the pre-art making stage of an art therapy session is setting therapeutic goals.[5] This is particularly important in the first session, but should also be followed up on in subsequent sessions. Treatment goals are typically discussed with the client to ensure that they are actively engaged in their own treatment plans and consequently feel that they have a purpose and sense of control over their circumstances.[5] In some cases, the pre-art making stage may actually include some art making if the therapist believes that the client would benefit from multiple art activities in a single session.[5]

The second stage of an art therapy session consists of the client making art. A number of factors are considered when deciding on an art activity for a given therapy session. Ultimately, the client's goals and comfort level with art are the factors that will determine the art form that the therapist chooses.[6] For instance, art therapists often choose magazine photo collages for people who are open to the idea of art therapy but are not yet comfortable with making art — choosing precut images and words feels much less intimidating than being asked to draw something from scratch.[6] Another consideration is whether the therapist will ask the client to create art based on an open theme of their own choosing, or if the therapist will prescribe a specific theme.[5] Again, the therapist's choice will depend on the goals of the therapy session and the particular outcomes that are desired. While the client is making their art, the therapist's role is primarily to observe, and perhaps take notes.[5] This process of observation has three main purposes: to study the client's process of art making, to provide assistance if needed, and to give the client the gift of one's full attention.[6] The art therapist's job during this time is not to act, inject, or judge, but merely to be present and attuned to the client, their art-making process, and their product. If the client has any questions or requires any assistance during this process, the therapist can offer their expertise to guide them. However, communication is typically non-directive during this time to avoid impinging on the client's freedom and creativity.[5]

The final, post-art making stage consists of discussing the art that the client has made. Once the client feels that their artwork is complete, the therapist may ask them to sit at a distance from the piece and observe it.[6] The reason for this is that the way that art looks sitting in front of the client can differ significantly from the way it looks from a distance.[6] This is one way in which art therapy offers the client a chance to see their issues from a new perspective.[6] The therapist will typically ask the client questions about their art and art-making process. During this stage, the therapist will often use some of the observations they made during the art making stage to explore the client's feelings and thoughts around the art activity.[5] One question that the therapist may ask the client is if they want to give their artwork a title.[5] This can prompt a discussion of how the client feels about their creation and pave the way for the client to summarize their thoughts and feelings and distill them to a central theme or issue to explore further.[5] Other questions that may arise during the discussion may include what the client thought about while making the artwork, what they thought about the materials they used, whether or not they noticed a chance in mood between the beginning of the activity and the end, and if the artwork stirred any memories or sparked any new ideas about their current circumstances.[5] After talking through the art-making process, the artwork, its meaning to the client, and the client's insights, the therapist may ask if they would change anything about the picture if they could, and invite them to make those changes.[6] Changing their artwork, which serves as a visual representation of their reality, acts as a proxy for the client to map out their path to change in real life.[6] Finally, once the session has ended, the therapist may wish to address how the artwork will be stored.[5] Art therapists often choose to keep clients' artwork with the therapist for the duration of the client's treatment, enabling them to refer to pieces in the future.[5]

Conclusion

Art therapy is a versatile therapeutic approach rooted in the long-standing connection between the creative process of making art and communication, self-expression, and healing. Research studies have yielded evidence supporting the efficacy of art therapy in the treatment of a variety of areas including substance use disorders, developmental disabilities, depression, anxiety, grief, trauma, and geriartric issues.[4] This approach can be used both as a stand-alone therapy and in conjunction with other therapeutic approaches such as cognitive behavioural therapy and group therapy.[1] Since its introduction as a formal practice in the 1940s, it has become a key form of expressive therapy with clients of all ages and from all walks of life benefiting from its healing potential.[2]

Chapter 3:

Art therapy

VS

other types of therapy

Written by Seonmin Jeong

Introduction

Therapy as a technique has widely been used as a method of treating patients with various mental illnesses and emotional challenges. Through the years, different types of therapy have been developed to treat such patients. Art therapy has risen in prominence to be one of them. Its technique helps patients cope with ideas or circumstances that they struggle to express verbally. It also helps them disconnect from their struggles by putting them on the page and talking about it. Metal health professionals have been incorporating art into their therapy sessions for a long time. However, there are still differences between traditional types of therapy and art therapy. In this chapter, the differences and similarities between art therapy and the four types of more traditional therapies will be explored.

What is art therapy

Art therapy is a technique that combines "the creative process and psychotherapy".[1] Like other therapies, this includes the patient and the therapist working through problems through verbal expression. However, art therapy also involves other materials and methods such as "imagery, colour and shape as part of this therapeutic process"[1]. This is a unique aspect of art therapy as the patient can express their feelings through various types of art. This is especially beneficial for the patient as he/she is able to express repressed or otherwise hard to explain feelings and thoughts through the unique mode of expression that is art.

The effectiveness of art therapy has been long debated. A review was conducted on literature published from 2000 to 2017[2]. It focuses on effectiveness of art therapy on adult clients and discusses the data collected from a research conducted by "non-certified art therapists or were restricted to a therapeutic intervention of a single session" in an environment that was not considered therapy.[2] Based on these findings, the literature review concludes that there is more work required to define and classify what exactly art therapy is.[2] However, the majority of data collected through this literature review shows that art therapy can have a positive impact on patients with various conditions.[2] Art therapy enhanced the quality of life of patients with various medical conditions.[2] However, the effectiveness of art therapy on patients with mental health issues varied. The research conducted throughout the years by medical professionals focused solely on adult patients with mental health issues, such as trauma or schizophrenia. For patients suffering from schizophrenia, the effectiveness of art therapy was found to be very low.[2] In the findings, it notes that the best way to approach treatment for schizophrenia is cognitive-behavioral therapeutic approach rather than art therapy.[2] For this reason, further research is needed to find ways to incorporate behavioral approach in art therapy.[2] Another widely diagnosed mental disorder is trauma. Most of the research conducted did not assess post-traumatic stress disorder, but rather, it was collected from case studies on patients who have experienced traumatic events.[2] Studies show that art therapy was beneficial when it was used over a longer period of time.[2] Art therapy was also effective for individuals dealing with everyday stress or burnout.[2] Some of the bias in this study includes lack of sufficient data and variability in each patient's circumstances.[2]

Pioneers of art therapy

Art therapy was introduced to Canada in the 1940s-1950s by Dr. Martin A Fisher, Selwyn and Irene Dewdney, and Marie Revai.[3] Dr Martin A. Fisher played a particularly big role in introducing art therapy to Canadian mental health professionals. He was the first to encourage his patients at Lakeshore Psychiatric hospital to use art. Later, he expanded the use of art therapy from adults to children, focusing on "the aspect of primary prevention of emotional problems"[3]. Likewise, Selwyn Dewdney began using art with psychiatric patients.[3] Marie Revai, on the other hand, began by teaching art to underprivileged children then after getting hired to work in the Allan Memorial Hospital, she used what she'd learned to incorporate art therapy into the treatment plans of psychiatric patients. [3]

Dr Fischer, one of the pioneers of art therapy, was particularly instrumental in discovering the potential of art therapy. In a session with a patient, he brought a pen and a pad for his patient to draw.[3] The next day, the patient came back with the pad filled with drawings.[3] This resulted in two things in terms of treatment for the patient. First, the patient showed a significantly lower level of stress after drawing.[3] Second, it acted as a tool that presented meaningful personal information to the therapist.[3] After this first encounter with art therapy, he continued using this technique with other patients. He became an advocate for the effects of art therapy and established the Toronto Art Therapy Institute.[3]

Selwyn Dewdney had a unique journey in establishing art therapy in the Western society. Mr. Dewdney and Ms. Dewdney were both very politically involved.[3] They fought to inform the general public of the importance of looking at psychiatric patients as people. After they were invited to Westminster Veteran's Hospital in London, Ontario as art therapists, they worked on the technique for twenty years.[3] At first, they started with no structure in art therapy. Patients were given materials to draw with and they had the freedom to draw whatever they wanted.[3] However, the Dewdneys slowly noticed that the patients were overwhelmed by the lack of structure.[3] They decided to develop a routine that supported the patients express more freely and calmly.[3]

Marie Revai had a similar story of becoming one of the pioneers of art therapy to the Dewdneys. She was an artist who had a teaching diploma from Budapest.[3] When she landed in Quebec with her sister, she started out working in factories. But she gets a new teaching job in Quebec city. There she taught at girls' summer camp and art museum in Montreal,

Quebec. This led her to being hired in the Occupational Therapy Department so she could teach art to psychiatric patients at the Alan Memorial Institute in Montreal.[3]

In Europe and North America, Freud's exploration of the unconscious had a significant impact on the idea of notion.[3] This sparked the idea that "not only dreams, but also art illustrates the unconscious".[3] This was largely spreading among two communities particularly, one being the professionals working with psychiatric patients and the other being the art teachers.[3] The psychiatric population believed that their patients were able to express or reveal their unconscious state through art. Art teachers noticed that the "art of their students was expressing very significant and meaningful personal issues which could be valuable in understanding human behavior"[3].

How to become 'art therapist' vs 'other therapist'

In Canada, there are only a handful of institutions that accept students into art therapy programs. "The Canadian Art Therapy Association only accepts professional or registered membership applicants from applicants who have graduated from an art therapy program that meets CATA's education standards".[4] These degrees typically take about 18 months to 2 years since they are frequently masters degree. The curriculum includes hands-on experience through placements, where students are provided the opportunity to engage with patients in hospitals, community centres, geeriatric facilities, or schools.[5] Moreover, it is a masters degree. The UK presents a similar process, the individual interested in becoming an art therapist must be registered with the Health and Care Professions Council (HCPC).[6] This usually takes two to four years. In East Asian countries such as Korea, students are also required to enrol in a masters degree in art therapy in order to practice as an art therapist.

In order to become a therapist that can perform therapies such as psychoanalysis, psychodynamic therapy, or dialectical behavior therapy, one needs to become either a psychiatrist, a psychologist, or a licensed professional counselor. Unlike with art therapists, becoming a psychiatrist requires the completion of a medical degree. As for psychologists, most acquire a Ph.D or a Psy.D. before beginning their practice. Licensed clinical social workers must complete thousands of supervised hours acquiring experience working with patients.[7] This differs from art therapists who require a mix of higher education and placement experience.

Art Therapy vs Other Therapies

The types of therapies can largely be divided into four categories. First, psychodynamic therapy refers to a "therapy developed from psychoanalysis, a long-term approach to mental health treatment".[8] Psychodynamic therapy requires therapist and patient to explore "the connection between your unconscious mind and your actions" often by conducting a series of detailed conversations whereas art therapy has a similar process but the conversation revolves around the artwork they've pronounced.[8]

Behavioral therapy is "a focused, action-oriented approach to mental health treatment".[8] This is done by focusing on changing the behavioral actions that cause distress through systematic desensitization, aversion therapy, or flooding.[8] The main difference between this type of therapy and art therapy is that art therapy only *explores* the patient's mind whereas behavioral therapy uses various methods in an attempt to *change* the patient's behavior..

Cognitive behavioral therapy (CBT) is "a short-term approach to mental health treatment". This type of therapy incorporates behavioral therapy by addressing "unhelpful thought patterns or problematic thoughts".[8] There are also sub categories of CBT. Dialectical behavioral therapy "prioritizes acceptance and emotional regulation".[8] Rational emotive therapy "helps you learn how to challenge irrational beliefs that contribute to emotional distress".[8]

Humanistic therapy is a type of therapy that focuses on the patient's world view. Since one's worldview can largely affect how one views one's own problems, it is important for therapists to guide the patients to a healthier worldview. Three sub categories of the humanistic therapy are existential therapy, person-centered therapy, and gestalt therapy.[8] Existential therapy helps the patient find greater meaning in life. Person-centered therapy is similar to art therapy in the sense that the patient is placed in a judgement free zone to express himself; it requires the therapist to show endless acceptance and empathy which can help the patient move forward from fear of judgement. Gestalt therapy "focuses on the present moment and often involves role-playing or acting out scenarios with movement or visualization"[8]. The visualization involved in this process is different from art therapy. This is because art therapy focuses on the patient expressing their unconscious state while the visualization used in gestalt therapy has its aim at the patient recognizing the true situation they are in.

Conclusion

The differences between art therapy and other types of therapy are clear. The process of becoming a therapist whether it is art therapist or other general therapists differs greatly, especially the length and the level of education it requires. Psychiatrists and psychotherapists both require more than a master's degree, whereas art therapists do not. Art therapy is also widely known around the world just like any other therapy programs. Uk, Korea, and Canada have a similar process in one becoming an art therapist. Most countries accept art therapy as a legitimate type of therapy. Although there are still differences in methods present between art therapy and other types of therapies, there are more similarities than differences.

Chapter 4:

Benefits of Art Therapy

Written by Khushi Shah

Art therapy is the concept of utilizing the creative process in the realm of psychotherapy in order to facilitate one's exploration and understanding of the self.[2] This is done through various forms of imagery, colour, shape and more, which can be seen as an outlet for one's inner thoughts and feelings through the therapeutic process that may otherwise be hard to articulate.[2] This type of therapy also allows for mental health to be explored through the active art-making creative process that can then be further analyzed through applied psychological theory. The types of practitioners that implement art therapy are licensed professionals with a master's degree as the minimum level of education with an additional 700 hours of clinical practicum in order to obtain an art therapist license.[2] Art therapy is conducted for individuals of all ages through personalized formats, group therapy sessions, family sessions, and/or couples counselling.[2] The goal of these therapy sessions is to improve the quality of life of the individual through a self-discovery process which enables the client to feel more in control of their lives as they are able to express their feelings in a safe space.[2] The therapy sessions occur under the guidance of an art therapist who is trained to encourage specific responses from the patient, as well as having the ability to analyze the artwork to promote the patient's mental health and well-being.[2] Some examples of the various forms of art therapy include but are not limited to painting, drawing, finger painting, working with clay, carving, sculpting, doodling, scribbling, making collages.[2]

Art therapy was first introduced in the 1940s by psychologists Margaret Naumburg and Edith Kramer.[6] These psychologists realized that allowing for the patient to communicate their feelings through creative expression combined with encouragement and verbal therapy helped the patients deal with intense emotions, increase self-awareness, increase self-worth, decrease stress, and decrease anxiety.[6] Research further demonstrated that this form of therapy is especially helpful for war veterans, prisoners, and individuals diagnosed with a mental disorder by a psychiatrist.[6] By the 20th century, art therapy had also become implemented into organizations beyond mental health facilities, including schools, shelters, nursing homes, residential old age homes,

and outpatient facilities.[6] By 2010, art therapy began to be used to treat
physical health difficulties as well. Researchers from Singapore found
that art therapy reduced the physical pain and decreased symptoms of
stress in adult cancer patients, it improved the ability of child cancer
patients to deal with pain, reduced stress and anxiety of children with
asthma, improved the overall quality of life of adults with dementia, and
reduced symptoms of depression in patients with Parkinson's disease.[6]

Art therapy has proven to have immensely positive results on children.
Parents and practitioners find that art therapy is able to conjure thoughts
and feelings of both the conscious and unconscious mind, allowing
for children to express themselves in a safe manner. Although, it is
important to note that art therapy is implemented in conjunction with
other therapy styles depending on the clients needs, the process of
creating pain healing, correcting, restoring, and resolving the patient's
needs.[1] These effects are similar to that of other psychotherapy practices,
but prove to have benefits when used in certain individuals and age
groups, one being children. Some of the benefits that researchers
have found art therapy has on children include promoting their self-
expression, feelings, and emotions.[1] Additionally, research shows that
children gain a greater positive perspective on life, build a stronger
sense of personal independence/self-reliance/ self-sufficiency, are better
able to work through difficult experiences they have had, allows children
to both verbally and nonverbally express emotions that they may have
difficulty communicating, helps children construct techniques to manage
their emotions, increases their awareness and increases orientation.[1]
Art therapy is extremely successful in its ability to facilitate and
develop strategies to improve physical health by improving the patient's
hand-eye coordination, motor skills, finger dexterity, and speed.[1] In
more recent years, clinical trials conducted with children undergoing
art therapy demonstrate that it positively encourages healthy coping
strategies, increases patients empathy/acceptance in other peoples life,
promotes one's problem-solving skills, increases children's insight
to aid in dealing with traumatic experiences, improves their ability to

develop interpersonal skills, gives children a safe space to voice their emotions, increases their attention span, and decreases them acting out due to frustrations.[1] All of these benefits found in children and early adolescents have been exhibited through multiple research and clinical studies. Case studies on the efficacy of art therapyinclude testing those with eating disorders, children struggling with emotional impairments, childhood grief, and sexual abuse survivors.[1] Research studies have also been conducted with adults struggling with addictions, patients undergoing bone marrow transplants, and families in bereavement.[1] These studies led to the findings that art therapy in patients reducing their stress levels, reduced anxiety levels, improved their recovery time over their respective illnesses, decreased the amount of time they need to spend in the hospital, improved their pain control, and strengthened patients social function (with on emphasis on their communication skills).[1]

A research study was conducted by Haeyen et al., in 2020 regarding the benefits of art therapy in people diagnosed with personality disorders.[3] This quantitative and practice-based study was completed over a period of three months by a self-report survey.[3] The survey contained 8 questions and 13 patients regarding the benefits they feel after implementing art therapy in their lives.[3] The total data was collected from 539 patients over the age of eighteen from which 27.1% were diagnosed with Cluster B personality disorder (95 participants had a borderline personality disorder and 2 had narcissistic personality disorder), 30.1% were diagnosed with a Cluster C personality disorder (95 participants have an avoidant personality disorder and 13 individuals had obsessive-compulsive personality disorder), and 34.5% had a non-specified personality disorder.[3] 78.6% of participants were female and overall the participants ranged from 19 years of age to 65.[3] The conclusions of the study indicate that patients believed that art therapy helped them improve in the aspects of expressing their emotions, improving their self-image, regained the ability to make their own choices (increased autonomy), improved insight, more strength

in dealing with their emotions, ability to deal with vulnerability, and improved change in the way patients are able to be aware of their emotions and implement productive coming strategies.[3] Patients also stated in their evaluations that their improvements increased after three months of art therapy. Compared to other methods of therapy, patients stated that art therapy makes them feel safer as there is no risk for judgmental attitudes of therapists. Patients felt like they were taken seriously, and they are given freedom of expression alongside being closely guided to help improve their quality of life.[3]
Researchers further concluded that since the effects of art therapy were equal throughout the age groups tested, this form of therapy is beneficial to the majority of the population and thus should be implemented more throughout therapy sessions.[3]

In a study conducted by Nainis et al., in 2006, the innovative use of art therapy to provide patients relief from cancer symptoms was studied. Fifty patients were a part of this study where all were over the age of 18. Individuals participated in one hour art therapy sessions weekly, were cognitively intact, and had a cancer diagnosis.[4] Out of all the participants 29.2% were diagnosed with leukemia, 32.6% had lymphoma, and they were all diagnosed 2-3 years prior to the study.[4] Around 88% of the participants had never participated in art therapy beforehand and after completing the study 92% of the participants (46 individuals) stated that they would continue to participate in art therapy.[4] The patients stated that their overall experience in the program was positive with 90% (45 individuals) of individuals stating the therapy session successfully distracted them from their pain and allowed them to focus on something more positive, 36% (18 individuals) of patients felt that it relaxed and calmed them down, 12% (6 individuals) of participants believed they felt more productive and worthwhile due to the sessions, 24% (12 individuals) of patients wanted to do more sessions weekly, and only 6% (3 individuals) of participants believed that the art therapy had no effects on them.[4] Furthermore, 96% of participants (48 individuals) stated that they felt comfortable when making art in the therapy sessions due to the comfort and guidance provided by the art therapist.[4] Overall, all participants stated that art made them feel more secure and in control of themselves and that they were able to express their thoughts and feelings without external pressure and the expectation to present their feelings verbally.[4] On the contrary, only 4% of participants (2 individuals) did not have positive progress from the art therapy but they also stated that this was due to them believing they had no skill or talent in that department, as well as did not like the final art pieces that they made.[4]

A study conducted by Sela et al., in 2007 explored how art therapy influenced depression and fatigue levels in cancer patients undergoing chemotherapy. The study was conducted with 60 cancer patients on chemotherapy who had to undergo weekly art therapy sessions, where they specifically only were allowed to paint with water-based colours.[5] Of the total 60 patients, 19 who participated in more than 4 art therapy sessions were analyzed as the experimental group and the other 41 who participated in two or fewer art therapy sessions became the control group.[5] The patients were tested based on the Hospital Anxiety and Depression Scale (also known as HADS) and the Brief Fatigue Inventory (also known as BFI) before each art therapy session and the results from each week were compared.[5] The results indicated that the Brief Fatigue Inventory scores were far higher in the control group than the experimental group.[5] Moreover, in the experimental group, the Brief Fatigue Inventory scores reduced from a 5.7 to a 4.1, the anxiety score of the patients significantly decreased from the pre-trial average, and the Hospital Anxiety and Depression Scale changed from a 9 to a 7 after around 4 art therapy sessions.[5] Given these results, the researchers were able to conclude that the depression, anxiety, and fatigue levels of all the patients did significantly decrease after only four weeks of art therapy.[5]

Further analysis on the effects of art therapy shows that it has the ability to help the disabled. Many disabled individuals find it difficult to communicate with others, which make it difficult to have day-to-day interactions and to seek employment.[7] The art therapy targeted for those with disabilities included painting with rich and vibrant colours which allowed the disabled individuals to communicate their feelings effectively without having to use verbal communication.[7] Furthermore, art therapy for the overall population aids in lowering their stress levels, allowing them to gain calmness and reprieve from any negative thoughts and/or behaviours.[7] Many describe this treatment style as a meditative form of therapy that forces one to concentrate on details in their own environment and express themselves as they choose.[7] Individuals often continue using strategies from rt therapy even after their sessions are complete as art itself has been proven to help people focus on improving their quality of work, which as a result positively improves their self-esteem.[7] Scientifically speaking, producing art enhances the body's neurotransmitter dopamine which is essentially the "feel-good" part of the nervous system as a result improving one's motivation, focus, drive, and concentration.[7] Art therapy also has been proven to enhance brain connectivity and the ability to increase intelligence practices as intelligence relies on the number of brain connections rather than the size of the connections.[7] Thus, art therapy can be scientifically proven to benefit one's quality of life and stimulate psychological resilience through the connections in the brain being increased, and behavioural outcomes.[7] Overall art therapy explores unresponsive emotions, improves one's mental/emotional health, has a positive effect on their physical health, and overall improves their quality of life.

Chapter 5:

Who is art therapy for?

Written by Anna Yang

Introduction

As is the case with all forms of therapy, not everybody benefits equally from art therapy. Groups that have been shown to benefit particularly greatly from art therapy include children, seniors, people who have experienced trauma, cancer patients, and people with mental health disorders such as depression and anxiety. This chapter will explore the benefits of art therapy for each of these groups in depth.

Art therapy for children

Children can benefit from art therapy in a number of ways and for a variety of reasons. Common uses of art therapy for youth include helping with behavioural issues, depression, anxiety, stress, attention deficit disorder/attention deficit hyperactivity disorder, autism spectrum disorder, learning disabilities, developmental disabilities, anger management, grief and loss, bullying or social isolation, trauma, attachment difficulties, and identity exploration.[1] One of the primary reasons that art therapy can be effective for children is that it is a non-verbal and sensory-based therapeutic approach which allows children to experience themselves and communicate on multiple levels, including visual, tactile, kinesthetic, and more.[2] As such, for children who are not able to effectively articulate their thoughts, emotions, or perceptions, art therapy provides a way for them to convey what is difficult to express with words.[2] For this same reason, art therapy can be particularly beneficial for children who have experienced abuse, as it is a way for them to "tell without talking" if they are unable or unafraid to speak about specific events or feelings.[2]

Art therapy can also provide a number of developmental benefits for children. One example of such a benefit is improving self-regulation. Certain sensory characteristics of the art-making process seem to be effective in improving mood and sensory integration while also helping to calm the body and mind.[2] This effect is especially pronounced in children who have experienced traumatic events.[2] Art therapy can also help with a child's social development, which is important as establishing social skills at a young age is a crucial aspect of regular development.[3] Evidence shows, for instance, that children who are comfortable in social settings are able to function more effectively as adults.[3] Art therapy can enhance a child's social development by providing them with support and an environment in which they are free from judgment from peers or parents.[3] Through discussions and interpretations of artwork, art therapy also gives children the chance to learn how to appreciate differences between people and to learn to accept different individuals' unique perspectives.[3] Finally, as with any type of therapy, interactions with the therapist can contribute to the development of a child's social skills, encouraging relationship-building and trust.[3] All creative arts therapies are inherently relational therapies because they involve an active, sensory-based dynamic between the therapist and the client.[2] As such, art therapy can be helpful in repairing and reshaping attachment through experiential means, allowing the child's brain to establish new, more productive patterns before unhealthy ones become firmly entrenched.[2]

Yet another developmental benefit that children can obtain from art therapy is improved cognitive development. Experiences in the arts go hand in hand with learning; through art, children can not only learn simple things like colours and shapes, but also obtain experiential lessons like cause and effect, choices and consequences, problem solving, experimenting, and decision-making.[3] On a cellular level, art has an impact on the brain's neural connections and affects the wiring that underlies learning processes.[3] Art-making requires deep thinking and the integration of the senses, which lead to the development of skills such as recognizing the difference between reality and the abstract, understanding patterns, making observations about the world, and forming mental representations of what is real or imagined.[3] Overall, the arts help children develop comprehensive thinking capabilities through the interactions of complex thought processes. In summary, art therapy can provide children with a number of benefits that help with the management of various disorders or illnesses, or which simply support and enhance a child's normal development.

Art therapy for seniors

Art therapy can have a number of positive effects for seniors as well. These include reducing stress and confusion, lowering the risk of depression, helping clients cope with traumatic memories, increasing cognitive function, increasing physical ability, promoting a sense of accomplishment through the creation of artwork, and promoting communication.[4] This section will explore some of the key benefits of art therapy for seniors in greater depth.

One way that art therapy can be beneficial for seniors is by enhancing their physical ability and motor skills. Studies have found that creating art can help promote coordination and decrease pain from conditions that commonly afflict the elderly, such as arthritis.[4] Particular art forms such as knitting, painting, and drawing can be especially beneficial for these purposes and can help seniors learn to more effectively use their hands while coping with chronic pain.[4] When people practice skills such as these in art therapy, they are physically exercising their hands and arms and, in doing so, can improve muscle coordination, enhance blood flow, and build better dexterity.[5]

Another significant benefit of art therapy for seniors is improving cognitive function. Through the challenge of making art, art therapy stimulates seniors' senses to become sharper.[5] Additionally, learning new art forms can enhance thinking skills and make it easier to make quick neural connections that may have eroded over time due to aging.[5] A related benefit is that art therapy can help improve memory. Studies have shown that making art can help seniors who suffer from memory loss caused by Alzheimer's or dementia by presenting them with moments of clarity.[5] In particular, painting and music may even help to uncover forgotten memories.[5] Additionally, art therapy can help patients with dementia to express themselves when other types of communication have deteriorated and no longer suffice.[6]

Art therapy can also help seniors by improving mood. Art therapy can reduce feelings of anxiety, depression, and stress in seniors, with studies showing that seniors who participate in creative arts experience lower levels of depression and loneliness.[5] Engaging in art therapy can help seniors better cope with the changes and issues that come with aging, such as hearing and vision loss, by providing them with a calming activity to focus on and also providing them with positive outlets for their frustration.[5] The social interaction that is a component of art therapy also plays a role in improving the emotional health of seniors. During art therapy sessions, seniors have the opportunity to meet like-minded people to interact and connect with on a regular basis.[5] These interpersonal connections can help combat loneliness and isolation.

Finally, art therapy can be beneficial for seniors by encouraging greater self-expression. Seniors may experience challenges with verbal communication due to mental or physical deterioration. Art therapy circumvents this by being a non-verbal approach and providing seniors with an alternative method of expression for their thoughts and feelings. Art therapists can guide seniors through artistic activities that allow them to freely express themselves, and this self-expression can help seniors learn how to better communicate with their caregivers and loved ones, ultimately improving their interpersonal relationships and emotional well-being.[5]

Art therapy for people with trauma

Another key demographic that art therapy has substantial benefits for is people who have experienced trauma and seek recovery from post-traumatic stress disorder (PTSD). PTSD is a psychiatric disorder that results from traumatic experiences and includes symptoms such as flashbacks, panic, anxiety, memory lapses, numbness, and dissociation.[7] According to Erica Curtis, a marriage and family therapist, "traumatic memories typically exist in our minds and bodies in a state-specific form, meaning they hold the emotional, visual, physiological, and sensory experiences that were felt at the time of the event. They're essentially undigested memories."[7] Consequently, recovering from PTSD requires working through these "undigested memories" until they no longer trigger PTSD symptoms. Common treatments for PTSD include talk therapy and cognitive behavioural therapy, both of which aim to desensitize the client by talking about the traumatic event and expressing the emotions associated with it.[7] However, verbal approaches such as these often aren't sufficient alone, and for certain individuals, may be quite limited in efficacy. For instance, research shows that over 30% of patients with PTSD do not benefit from trauma-focused cognitive behavioural therapy or other evidence-based treatments such as eye movement desensitization and reprocessing.[8] For patients with prolonged and multiple traumatization, poor verbal memory, or emotional over-modulation, retelling traumatic experiences is poorly tolerated and verbal treatments such as talk therapy or cognitive behavioral therapy are often not completed.[8] Here, art therapy proves particularly useful as it helps patients process traumatic events in a new way. The nonverbal and experiential nature of art therapy makes it an effective approach for addressing the often wordless and visual nature of traumatic memories; by addressing images rather than words, it offers a different kind of access to traumatic memories and emotions which is more tolerable to patients who are unable to talk about traumatic memories and unable to tolerate exposure treatments.[8]

PTSD recovery also involves reclaiming the safety of one's body. Many who live with PTSD find themselves disconnected from their bodies as the result of having felt threatened and physically unsafe during traumatic events.[7] As such, learning to have a relationship with one's body is a critical component of recovering from PTSD. Bessel van der Kolk, author of *The Body Keeps the Score*, noted that "traumatized people chronically feel unsafe inside their bodies. In order to change, people need to become aware of their sensations and the way that their bodies interact with the world around them. Physical self-awareness is the first step in releasing the tyranny of the past."[7] Art therapy excels in this department because it gives clients the opportunity to manipulate artwork outside of themselves. By externalizing components of their trauma, clients begin to learn how to safely access their physical experiences and relearn that their bodies are a safe place.[7] Patients who participate in art therapy often report feeling uplifted, free to step away from their traumatic experiences during the process, and more mindful of the behaviours that result from these intense feelings.[9]

A number of studies have yielded evidence that supports the efficacy of art therapy as a treatment for PTSD. For instance, a pilot study in the Netherlands examined the effect of a trauma-focused art therapy protocol on PTSD symptom severity and found that patients reported beneficial effects such as increased relaxation, the externalization of memories and emotions into artwork, fewer intrusive thoughts of traumatic experiences, and greater confidence in the future.[8] The study found art therapy to be particularly useful for patients with multiple and prolonged traumatization, such as patients with early childhood traumatization, and for refugees and asylum seekers from different cultural backgrounds since art therapy could bridge language and cultural gaps.[8] Other studies have analyzed children with PTSD and found that those who participate in art therapy often see a reduction in their acute symptoms.[10] Art therapy has also been found to be an ideal way to reach treatment-resistant teens who are reluctant to engage in talk therapy. Shirley Riley, an art therapist in Los Angeles, says that art is amenable to teens because "adolescents are attracted to making symbols and graphic depictions" more than they are to verbal question and answer sessions.[10]

Art therapy for cancer patients

Art therapy has been shown to be helpful to cancer patients at multiple different stages of illness, especially during isolation for bone marrow transplantation, during radiotherapy treatment, and after treatment.[11] Although there is no evidence that art therapy can treat cancer itself, it has been found that people living with cancer, their partners, and their family members may benefit from using art therapy as a way of helping them deal with their emotions.[12] While scientific evidence in this area is still relatively limited, many health professionals believe that art therapy may help cancer patients express their emotions, improve their relationships with other people, adjust to a changing body image, take their minds off their pain or discomfort, and control their anxiety, depression, or low self-esteem.[13] Research has shown that art therapy can be particularly useful in helping children and teens communicate how they feel about their cancer and treatment.[12]

While it is generally agreed to additional research on the effectiveness of art therapy for cancer patients is still required, the evidence that currently exists is promising nonetheless. For instance, a study by the National Institutes of Health that involved 1500 participants found that art therapy helped to reduce anxiety, depression, and physical pain in patients, with most patients reporting a general improvement in their quality of life.[14] This research suggested that the emotional benefits lasted as long as the therapy itself, but reduction in pain was observed in patients after the therapy ended as well.[14] Another study examining how women receiving radiation treatment for breast cancer could benefit from art therapy found that their overall health improved, along with their quality of life, physical health, and psychological health.[14] They also had better body image, were better able to cope with the physical side effects of treatment, and felt more hopeful about the future.[14]

Art therapy for people with mental health disorders

Depression

While traditional methods of treating depression, such as talk therapy and medication, are often effective for many people, alternative treatments like art therapy continue to gain popularity.[15] People who struggle with depression may have a difficult time articulating their feelings, and as such, art therapy provides these people with an alternative way to express themselves, as well as an opportunity to slow down and explore the issues that are occurring in their life. Through art therapy, people can experience profound benefits not found through other therapeutic approaches, such as finding a means of expression that does not require verbal communication. As Douglas Mitchel, a marriage and family therapist, has noted, "it can be difficult to open up to complete strangers about your deepest darkest emotions. Sometimes we are taught to suppress our emotions and put on a blank face, even when experiencing inner turmoil." Art therapy circumvents these obstacles and allows one to achieve a sense of independence and self-sufficiency, break through dysfunctional thought patterns, develop healthy coping mechanisms, and strengthen one's problem-solving skills.[16]

Convincing evidence exists in support of the efficacy of art therapy for people with depression. A meta-review published in 2015 examining the impact of art therapy on depression reported that "patients receiving art therapy had significant improvements in 14 out of 15 randomized control trails."[16] Another study found that people with depression who participate in art therapy "make less phone calls to medical and mental health providers; require fewer referrals to medical specialists; have a decreased number of somatic symptoms and complaints; and reduce their utilization of medical and mental health services."[16] Furthermore, a study by the University of Gothenburg in 2017 found a clear effect of art therapy on severe depression.[17] After ten hour-long sessions of art therapy, patients suffering from severe or moderately severe depression showed more improvements than patients in the control group.[17] It is worth noting, however, that the patients in the study were not given art therapy as a standalone treatment; instead, art therapy was administered in combination with medication, cognitive behavioural therapy, psychodynamic therapy, and physical therapy.[17] Current research shows that art therapy is most effective when incorporated within a broader range of therapeutic interventions to create a comprehensive treatment experience for people with depression.[16]

Anxiety

People with anxiety are often overwhelmed with negative thoughts and worry. As such, the intention behind art therapy for people with anxiety is to interrupt and distract them from these thoughts and emotions that threaten to overwhelm them.[18] Research has shown that art therapy has a number of benefits for people with anxiety. One benefit is that art therapy calms the nervous system. Art therapy activities are meditative, quiet, and calming, which helps soothe stress, nervousness, and irritability. A calm mind is better able to process difficult emotions and experiences, and consequently, art therapy can help patients resolve deep inner conflicts through meaningful moments of calm.[19] Another benefit is that art therapy can help increase one's self-awareness. As a patient engages in creative pursuits, they are often able to discover new aspects of themselves that they weren't aware of before.[19] As such, it is much easier to understand the feelings and thoughts that exist below the surface of one's conscious mind when focusing on a creative activity, as one does in an art therapy session.

While research in this area is relatively limited, some studies have yielded evidence of art therapy's efficacy in supporting people with anxiety. One such study examined the effectiveness of art therapy on anxiety in adult women between 18 and 65 years of age.[20] All of the participants were diagnosed with generalized anxiety disorder, social anxiety disorder, or panic disorder, with moderate to severe anxiety symptoms.[20] Analyses of the data demonstrated that the group that underwent art therapy showed a reduction in anxiety, an increase in subjective quality of life, and an improvement in accessibility of emotion regulation strategies compared to the control group.[20] Treatment effects remained after 3 months of follow-up, suggesting that art therapy has long-lasting positive effects for people with anxiety.[20]

Conclusion

Art therapy benefits different groups to varying extents and in unique ways. While the efficacy of art therapy generally remains an area in need of further research, there already exists some research demonstrating the benefits of art therapy for specific groups, namely children, seniors, people who have experienced trauma, cancer patients, and people with mental health disorders such as depression and anxiety.

Chapter 6

The science behind Art Therapy

Written by Terrence Wu

Introduction to Art Therapy

Art therapy has become increasingly common in treating patients with neuropsychiatric disorders. Within the field of neuroscience, the study of the brain and its function, the goal of practicing and promoting art therapy is to gain acceptance and credibility from the medical establishment.[1] According to the American Art Therapy Association (2019), art therapy integrates mental health and human services, with the ultimate goal of enriching the lives of individuals, families, and communities. This is done using a variety of methods, including "active art making, creative process/theory, applied psychological theory, and human development with a psychotherapeutic relationship".[2] A trained art therapist is able to use art therapy to facilitate a therapeutic relationship with the patient. Art therapy has become an integral part of many types of psychiatric treatment plans. Art therapists build and support therapeutic relationships by using "a range of artistic media intervention strategies to engage the client in creative expression with the aim of symptom reduction".[2] In many aspects, art therapy is considered "reparative and adaptive because it taps into the creative and imaginative aspects of human brain functioning".[2]

The processes surrounding the creation and production of visual art are "deeply embedded in human nature across races and cultures from the early history of civilization".[3] Studies have shown that humans use artistic expression to evoke different types of "emotions and imagination, stimulating cognition, and, enabling communication".[2] Additional investigatory studies currently being conducted have shown that individuals living with different mental illnesses often best express themselves using drawings and other forms of artistic expression. This observation has led to further research being done regarding the use of art as a healing strategy to support a patient's quality of life.[4] Scientific methods are currently used and required, in order to validate art therapy models. Future research needs to be done on examining the effects of art therapy on brain function, which leads to the study of brain imaging. Further research is looking at establishing the effects of art therapy on specific brain structures.[1]

Types of Art and Creative Therapies

There are many types of artistic and creative therapies that can be used in the treatment of a mental illness.[4] Therapeutic interventions and examples of these practices include dance therapy, drama therapy, expressive therapy, and music therapy, which will be discussed in further detail.

Dance therapy, also known as Dance Movement Therapy (DMT), is proven to be an effective intervention in facilitating the treatment of depression in adults. DMT can help mitigate some of the negative symptoms associated with depression, including distress, functional impairment, low mood, low motivation, sleep disturbances, changes in appetite and body weight, decreased energy, slowed or agitated movement, low concentration, feelings of guilt and worthlessness, and thoughts of suicide.[5] However, further evidence from meta-analyses need to be gathered in order to ensure that the current research surrounding the effects of DMT is consistent across translational research findings to the stages of clinical practice.[5]

Drama therapy can be used in the treatment of "motivated, neurotic clients in individual psychotherapy".[6] The aim of drama therapy is to "emphasize the use of developmental sequences of dramatic forms to facilitate a spontaneous flow of images within the client".[6] There are many factors that contribute to building dramatic forms, which includes overall structure, complexity, media, interpersonal demand, and expression of affect. In a clinical and therapeutic setting, the therapist introduces small variations in these forms which creates character and evolves the imaginative process for the client. This exercise may also be used to facilitate group therapy sessions, which can increase overall interest within a group as compared to using a pre-set sequence of planned exercises. These therapeutic sessions can further develop in "stages of unison movement and sound, definition of images, personification into roles, structured role-playing, and unstructured role-playing".[6]

Expressive therapy is commonly used to treat younger patients, where they have been severely maltreated during their childhood or upbringing. There are many clinical implications for using expressive therapy. This non-verbal approach is proven to be highly effective because it does not rely on the client's use of their left brain and language for processing.[7] It has been shown that non-verbal, expressive therapies are more effective than verbal therapies — particularly when it comes to treating children experiencing difficulties with attachment. Children who have poor attachment skills or those that have experienced trauma during their lifetime may have certain deficits in brain development.[7] It has been found that histories of traumatic attachment affect the development of the frontolimbic regions of the brain. Specifically, this includes the areas of the right cortical areas that are involved in affect-regulating functions.[7]

Music therapy is used to improve the psychological and physiological health of individuals. There are five factors that contribute to the effects of music therapy: attention, emotion, cognition, behaviour, and communication.[8] The first factor is attention, as music has the ability to quickly draw attention away from individuals. Because music is so captivating to human ears, music can be used to distract patients from stimuli in their environment that may provoke negative experiences. These negative stimuli can include pain, anxiety, worry, and sadness.[8] The second factor is emotion, which was discovered through functional neuroimaging. Music affects the major limbic and paralimbic brain structures, which are areas that are directly involved in the initiation, generation, and modulation of emotions.[8] The third factor is cognition, which links together the associations between memory processes and music. The brain is responsible for building memory capacity through encoding, storage, and decoding information. The brain mentally links events that are associated with music and analyzes the musical contents to determine syntax and music meaning.[8] The fourth factor is behaviour, which describes different movement patterns associated with musical therapeutic effects, such as walking, speaking, grasping, etc.[8] The fifth and final factor is communication. Music therapy can be used as an active form of therapy, where patients are creating music in the moment. This communicative factor of music therapy allows therapists to treat clients with communication disorders and for those with interpersonal competencies.[8]

Exploring the realms of art therapy

Using the scientific method, researchers can further investigate the realms of visual art and art therapy. A great deal of current research surrounds areas of interest, including how participating in art therapy sessions affects the brain's physiology and structure of a patient. The aim of gathering these results is to extrapolate the evidence to support how art therapy can create a more flexible and adaptable individual.[1] Through furthering our neurological understanding of art therapy, one of the main goals of research is to identify particular brain areas of activity patterns that are directly linked to the process of creating art.[1,3]

Electroencephalograms, commonly abbreviated as EEGs, are used to diagnose changes or abnormalities in brain waves. The EEG test measures the amount of electrical activity in the brain. In this process, small metal disks, known as electrodes, are connected to a series of wires which are placed on the scalp of the head. These electrodes are used to measure the activity of the brain cells by detecting small changes in electrical signals.[9] Synchronization is described as a "a basic mechanism for neuronal information processing within a brain area as well as for communication between different brain areas supporting maximum functional permissiveness".[3]

In the practice of art therapy, EEG phase synchrony analysis is used to study visual perception, by examining the functional and topographic differences between groups of patients. Phase synchrony is a result of "context-dependent, dynamical co-operations between multiple cortical areas".[3] Bottom-up processing is associated with synchrony that is observed in higher frequencies. However, when patients are characterized as using top-down processing to solve problems, it was found that their "actual mental sensory experience is produced by exclusively internal activation, large-scale convergence takes place between multiple cortical areas, which might be mediated by the enhanced phase relationships in very low frequency bands".[3] This large-scale cortical integration is supported by the anatomy and evidence of these observed cortical areas being extremely interconnected by reciprocal cortico-cortical and subcortical pathways.[3]

The Importance of Visual Perception

Visual perception can be divided into three main steps. The first stage includes basic feature analysis, which accounts for different shapes, forms, colours, contours, and contrasts, etc. This feature analysis is primarily processed within the primary visual cortex.[3] The second stage is the organization of the primary information into fundamental and coherent forms. This is commonly done through visual discriminatory processes, and figure-ground analysis.[3] The third stage involves giving these fundamental forms meaning through associations with previous knowledge that is already stored in long-term memory.[3]

Visual cognition is broken down into two distinct stages, known as bottom-up processing and top-down processing. Multiple studies have shown that visual perception is encoded by different areas within the primary visual cortex. Area V1 encodes bottom-up processing, while area V2 is responsible for encoding top-down processing. In addition, area V4 bridges the encoding gap between areas V1 (bottom-up) and V4 (top-down).[10] Understanding the distinction between bottom-up and top-down processing is based on three main factors. The first factor states that information processing is organized hierarchically. The second factor describes how lower levels of the hierarchy represent detailed stimulus information, while higher levels represent more integrated information. The third and final factor states that information exchange between levels is bidirectional.[10] There are many distinct ways and thought processes that are used to understand top-down processing. Top-down processing is typically viewed as cognitive operations which lead to comprehension.[3] One such perspective is derived from an anatomical standpoint, which equates top-down processes with functional activity along descending connections between the levels of the hierarchy. There is a cognitivist perspective, which views top-down thinking practices as hypothesis-driven processing. A gestaltist perspectives sees top-down processes in terms of contextual modulations of bottom-up processing. Lastly, the dynamicist perspective describes top-down processes in terms of an entrainment of local neuronal populations by widespread oscillatory activity in distant and distributed brain regions.[10]

The brain becomes influenced by external factors, including "artistic education background, abilities, personalities, good visual memory, pronounced interest in cultures, etc".[3] The brain receives feedback from many external processes. This can come from outside stimuli that may be competing for the viewer's attention to specific parts of the visual object, which is a process known as binding. This process gives more importance to salient features based on personal inclinations and experiences. The brain uses this information to incorporate raw visual impressions into the primary visual cortex, which adds a richness of meaning that is far more in-depth and beyond the scope of the original input stimuli.[3] Art therapists can use this knowledge to facilitate better therapeutic interventions to incorporate a patient-centered care experience for these individuals undergoing art therapy.

Neuroimaging Research in Art Therapy

There are many widespread impacts of imaging the brain. Neuroimaging allows for the evaluation of brain functioning from a variety of perspectives.[1] Research has shown that there are structural brain differences between individuals with various neurological disorders, including schizophrenia and autistic spectrum disorders. These studies have drawn associations and made connections stating that the structure of the brain areas are related to function, which leads to the onset of symptoms that patients will most likely experience during their lifetime with the disorder. However, it is important to account for the fact that structural anomalies do not always cause symptoms. Similarly, scientists cannot make the association that symptoms drive the development of abnormal brain structures. However, it can be said that "the brain's structure changes as a consequence of illness and activity".[1]

Conclusion

Current and future research is looking at unraveling scientific explanations that explain the benefits of art therapy supporting a variety of neurological and psychiatric disorders. There are many types of art and creative therapies that are used in clinical settings to facilitate treatment plans for patients of all types. Art therapy is seen to have an expansive potential in building and facilitating long-lasting therapeutic relationships between the patients and the art therapist. The study of art therapy is focused on gaining the attention of solidified scientific evidence, which stems around better understanding how visual perception and neuroimaging research play into explaining the effectiveness of art therapy.

Chapter 7:
Current and future research

Written by Ashmita Mazumder

When applying any intervention, it is important to establish its effectiveness in specific clinical populations. In this chapter, we will briefly look at past research on art therapy, which will inform our discussion on current and future research in the field. In doing so, we will look at the most influential studies in the field through different systematic reviews conducted from the 1970s when the field was formalized, to the present day. Systematic reviews are published research papers that collect and summarize empirical evidence on a research question. These reviews are especially useful when looking at the effectiveness of an intervention as they outline research by multiple authors and analyze the combined effectiveness of the proposed intervention while considering factors such as age, research design, effect size etc. Therefore, they are an excellent resource to critically evaluate the results and identify limitations of the existing literature.

A Brief Review of Past Research

1971-2000

Most research conducted in the field of art therapy before 1999 focused on case studies.[15] While case studies can help in illustrating theories and generating new ideas, they cannot be used as evidence in determining the effectiveness of a particular intervention, as they are subjective accounts and are not generalizable to larger group. Other research has focused on theoretical concepts that laid the foundation for future studies. In 1999, Reynolds and colleagues published a systematic review of the literature on the effectiveness of art therapy.[16] The authors defined art therapy as the "practice that involves the application of knowledge about human emotional, social, and behavioral development".[16] They found seventeen published articles that had looked at the effectiveness of art therapy on a treatment group. The authors then categorized the studies into three groups: studies with no control group, controlled clinical trial designs, and randomized clinical trial designs.

Eight of the seventeen studies identified belonged to the first category: studies with no control group. Out of these eight studies, seven found a decrease in symptomatology and improvement from behavioral problems after art therapy was implemented, while one found no changes in symptomatology.[16] Studies reported an increase in self-esteem after four weeks of therapy, improvement in global health, and improvement in anxiety-depression scores. However, results from such studies should be interpreted with caution. Due to the absence of a control group which did not receive the therapy, it is difficult to conclude that the improvements were due to the therapy alone and not some extraneous variable.

Four of the seventeen studies identified belonged to the category of controlled (nonrandomized) studies.[16] Two of these studies found significant improvements in those that received art therapy. These improvements include reduction in the level of depression, and improvement in catharsis and cohesion. However, in this research design participants are not randomly assigned to groups. Random assignment to groups is important to ensure that participant variables do not interfere with the results of the study. For example, the researcher's decision to assign the first fifteen people that arrive to one group and the other fifteen to another can have serious implications on the result of the study as the ones that arrive first may be systematically different from the ones that arrive later. Therefore, not randomly assigning them into groups has the possibility of amplify their differences such that any results from these studies could become difficult to interpret.

Finally, the authors reported five randomized controlled trials. Among these studies, three found significant improvements in the group that received art therapy. Improvements include increased social peer-related self-esteem, increase in self-concept, and better attitudes towards self. Randomized control trials allow for random assignment into groups and have a control group that does not receive any intervention. Therefore, we can be confident about the results found in such studies.

The studies published up to the year 2000 provide substantial evidence in support of art therapy. However, there are several problems regarding the research design of these studies which were highlighted in the paper by Reynolds et al. and motivated future research in the field.

2000-2010

The time between the years 2000 and 2010 saw a substantial increase in the interest and an improvement in the research quality on art therapy.[11]

An influential study from this period published by Ball in 2002 prompted an in-depth discussion on the attachment needs of children who have experienced trauma and how art therapy can be a way of self-regulation for them.[1] The study found that after undergoing art therapy for six months and in conjunction with several interactions with the therapist, there were significant changes in how the children processed the traumatic experiences. The authors also reported that children were able to symbolize their experiences through art which could help in the regulation of emotions and impulses.[1] However, this study documented case studies, as the "data collection" involved the author being present as an observer while a therapist conducted her sessions with a particular client. Hence, there are issues with the generalizability of the results.

Another influential study by Lyshak-Stelzer et al. in 2007 studied the effectiveness of art-therapy in a trauma-focused setting.[10] The participants for this study were hospitalized adolescents who were being treated for post-traumatic stress disorder. The authors found significant symptom reduction in the sample following two years of art therapy. Given the experimental design of the study, we can be more confident about the effectiveness of the intervention for the sample and the generalizability of the results.

In 2008, Slayton et al. published a meta-analysis as a direct response to the concerns raised in the paper published by Reynolds in 2000.[18] In comparison to Reynolds et al. in 2000 which only found 17 articles that fit their inclusion criteria, Slayton and colleagues found 35 studies published from 2000-2008 that investigated the effectiveness of art therapy as a measurable outcome. Out of these 35 studies, they found 11 studies that had experimental designs with random assignment. This was an improvement from Reynolds et al. that only found five studies with this design[18] Although the number is still considerably small, it suggested that researchers were making an effort to strengthen the confidence in their results by implementing better research designs. Eight out of the eleven studies found improvement in symptomatology in the group that received art therapy compared to the group that did not. The authors of the review report that there is substantial evidence in support of art therapy improving a variety of symptoms for a variety of people from different age groups.

However, the body of research still had its shortcomings. There were few studies that had tested the effectiveness of art therapy on children and while the number of studies with control groups and proper research designs had gone up, there was still a long way to go.

Several papers between 2010 to 2020 have started to focus on evaluating the effectiveness of art therapy on specific populations.[12] Past research in the field has looked at the effectiveness of art therapy on diverse populations ranging from children to adults and even clinical populations such as patients with cancer or depression. A natural extension of this line of research is to conduct an in-depth investigation testing the effects of art therapy on specific clinical samples.

Cancer Patients

Most studies that have discussed the results of art therapy on cancer patients have only administered the therapy for less than a few months. However, one such study by Monti et al. in 2012 incorporated fMRI measurements along with the intervention.[14] Researchers found that art therapy improved physical symptoms along with life satisfaction, depression, anxiety and fatigue.[14] The authors also reported that short term interventions in the form of art therapy can improve patients' coping mechanisms, emotional state and perceived symptoms. Further research is needed in order to determine the long-term effects of art therapy on cancer patients.

Patients with Other Medical Conditions

The earliest study that dealt with art therapy on clients that did not have cancer was conducted in 2011 by Sela and colleagues.[17] The study had a small sample size of only 20 participants who partook in art therapy for six weeks, and were diagnosed with advanced heart failure. The study employed a randomized controlled trial approach and found that patients that underwent art therapy were able to express their emotions better and their scores on general life satisfaction also improved.[17] Similarly, another study in 2014 investigated the effect of art therapy on patients suffering from HIV/AIDS.[6] This study did not have any control groups and patients received art therapy in individual or group settings for one or more sessions. The authors found significant improvements in depression severity scores and quality of life scores for patients. However, due to the lack of a control group, the results are vulnerable to confounding effects.

Mental Health

A study by Crawford et al. in 2012 discusses the effectiveness of art therapy on individuals with schizophrenia.[5] The study had a fairly large sample size of 159 patients who were randomly assigned to either receive art therapy (intervention group) or attend group activities (control group). The patients attended weekly therapy sessions for 90 minutes for an average period of 12 months. This longitudinal study did not find any differences in scores in the global functioning or quality of life scales between the group that received art therapy compared to the group that did not.[5] Similarly, another randomized study by Leurent et al. in 2014 that looked at patients with schizophrenia did not find any differences between the group that received art therapy and the group that did not.[8] Another study by Chandraiah et al. in 2012 addressed the effectiveness of art therapy for women coping with depression.[4] This study found significant improvements in depressive symptoms after patients underwent at least eight therapy sessions. However, this study did not include a control group.

The Elderly

The effectiveness of art therapy on the elderly has been studied at length. One study was conducted on Korean American older individuals in 2013.[7] This study involved randomization where one group underwent twelve art therapy sessions, each lasting between 60-75 minutes, and the other group did not receive any intervention. The participants in the art therapy group showed significant improvements in positive affect and decreases in both state and trait anxiety. These participants also showed an increase in self-esteem after the intervention. Another study dealt with older adults coping with depression.[13] This study also involved randomization and patients either underwent six weeks of art therapy (twice a week) or no intervention at all. The authors found significant decreases in depressive symptoms in patients that underwent art therapy compared to the group that did not receive therapy.

Children and Youth

The effectiveness of art therapy on children and youth is probably the most widely studied population. A published systematic review on this topic found 1299 studies that had measured the outcomes of art therapy on children.[3] A particularly influential paper in this group was by Bazargan and Pakdaman in 2016.[2] The sample in this study consisted of sixty participants whose ages ranged from fourteen to eighteen. Youth in this sample showed signs of problematic internalizing and externalizing behavior. The participants underwent six group art therapy sessions which lasted for sixty minutes each. The authors found a significant decrease in internalizing behavior although no significant changes were found in externalizing behavior.[2] Similarly, another influential paper written by Liu in 2017 addressed the effectiveness of art therapy on children that underwent traumatic experiences and self-reported sleep-related problems.[9] The ages of participants ranged from six to thirteen and they were given eight group art therapy sessions in two weeks. The author found a decrease in trauma and sleep related symptoms.[9]

The above categorizations outline the discrepancies in results within the field. While the effects of the intervention are well studied in children, much research is needed to confidently approach other populations such as those with mental health conditions or cancer. Throughout the years there has been a significant improvement in the quality of studies published as well as an increase in the number of studies being published. We have seen a considerable shift from studies with no control group to randomized controlled trials with an emphasis on producing generalizable results. However, much more research is needed in the field to confidently list art therapy as a successful intervention.

Future Research

The American Art Therapy Association (AATA) was established in 1999 as an attempt to encourage research on art therapy.[19] Even though the earliest study that looked at the effectiveness of art therapy was published in 1971, the number and quality of studies on art therapy increased after the introduction of the AATA. Today, the AATA runs a peer-reviewed journal that publishes research by professional art therapists or research related to art therapy from around the world. The association's website also contains resources for aspiring art therapists and information about guidelines on how to practice art therapy. Moreover, the organization outlines different guidelines for research in this field and lays the foundations for future directions in the field.

The AATA recommends that researchers focus on research areas such as the outcomes/efficacy of art therapy.[19] For example, the organization seeks to address which interventions produce specific outcomes on particular populations or specific disorders. Secondly, they encourage researchers to understand associations between art therapy and neuroscience and the processes and mechanisms involved in art therapy. For example, addressing the neurobiological processes involved in art making during art therapy. Next, they aim to address the assessment, validity and reliability of art therapy by investigating the validity and reliability of art therapy assessments and comparing the techniques used to other therapeutic disciplines that do not incorporate art.

Finally, the organization aims to establish directions for cross-cultural approaches to art therapy.[19] For example, determining how art therapy can be made more effective for people from different racial and ethnic backgrounds. In addition to outlining future directions for research, the organization also suggests populations of interest where research is recommended which include veterans, people with major psychiatric mental illness, people on the autism spectrum, people with medical conditions such as cancer, at-risk youth in schools, and geriartric individuals. Researchers should use the guidelines provided on this website to inform further studies.

Conclusion

Research on the effectiveness of art therapy began as early as 1971. From this point forward, work in this field has improved how art therapy is applied and more importantly, has informed clinicians about populations that show significant improvements after receiving art therapy. From 1971 to 1999, there were many studies that only reported case studies or only studied the effects of art therapy on one group without comparing it to the outcomes in a control group. However, this methodology was improved in subsequent years as more and more

studies started to randomize assignment into groups and included a
control group. This was an important step towards establishing results
in the field, as studies without control groups are vulnerable to multiple
variables that affect results. Today, the field has made significant
improvements in terms of methodology and emphasis on specific
samples. Researchers have started to shift their focus on testing the
effectiveness of the intervention on clinical populations of all ages.
Throughout this, the American Art Therapy Association remains the
guiding light for researchers, providing not only resources on art therapy
but also a chance for the publication of research on this topic, allowing
for better communication of results.

References

Works Cited (Chapter 1)

How to journal: Top 3 mistakes when starting a journal. (2016, February 8).

A quote by Pablo Picasso. (n.d.). Goodreads.Com. Retrieved July 30, 2021, from https://www.goodreads.com/quotes/4673-art-washes-away-from-the-soul-the-dust-of-everyday

Levine, S. K. (2015). The Tao of poiesis: Expressive arts therapy and Taoist philosophy. *Creative Arts in Education and Therapy*, *1*(1), 15–25.

Moss, R. C., & Perryman, K. L. (2012). East meets west: Integration of Taoism into Western therapy. *American Counseling Association VISTAS*, *46*(4), 1-12.

Waller, D. (2013). *Becoming a profession: The history of art therapy in Britain 1940-82*. Routledge. https://doi.org/10.4324/9780203750209

Wilde, O. (1997). *The Soul of Man Under Socialism*. Project Gutenberg.

Wikipedia contributors. (2021, July 15). *Vienna Secession*. Wikipedia, The Free Encyclopedia. https://en.wikipedia.org/w/index.php?title=Vienna_Secession&oldid=103380084

The why and how of art therapy. (2020, June 24).

Brown, A. D. (2012, February 28). *Psychological benefits of art therapy - Canadian counselling and psychotherapy association*. Ccpa-Accp.Ca. https://www.ccpa-accp.ca/psychological-benefits-of-art-therapy/

Kopytin, A., & Lebedev, A. (2013). Humor, self-attitude, emotions, and cognitions in group art therapy with war veterans. *Art Therapy: Journal of the American Art Therapy Association*, *30*(1), 20–29.

Works Cited (Chapter 2)

Cherry K. How art therapy works [Internet]. Verywellmind.com. [cited 2021 Jul 27]. Available from: https://www.verywellmind.com/what-is-art-therapy-2795755

Dresden D. Art therapy: Definition, uses, and how it works [Internet]. Medicalnewstoday.com. 2020 [cited 2021 Jul 27]. Available from: https://www.medicalnewstoday.com/articles/art-therapy

Rubin JA. What is art therapy? In: Introduction to Art Therapy. Routledge; 2009. p. 25–48.

What is art therapy? — Canadian art therapy association [Internet]. Canadianarttherapy.org. [cited 2021 Jul 27]. Available from: https://www.canadianarttherapy.org/what-is-art-therapy

What happens in an art therapy session [Internet]. Com.au. 2017 [cited 2021 Jul 27]. Available from: https://arttherapyresources.com.au/happens-art-therapy-session/

What is an Art Therapy Session Like? [Internet]. Mindfulartstudio.com. [cited 2021 Jul 27]. Available from: https://mindfulartstudio.com/what-is-an-art-therapy-session-like/

Works Cited (Chapter 3)

What is art therapy? — Canadian art therapy association. (n.d.). Retrieved August 14, 2021, from Canadianarttherapy.org website: https://www.canadianarttherapy.org/what-is-art-therapy

Regev, D., & Cohen-Yatziv, L. (2018). Effectiveness of art therapy with adult clients in 2018-what progress has been made? *Frontiers in Psychology*, *9*, 1531.

(N.d.). Retrieved August 14, 2021, from Lizmcknight.com website: http://lizmcknight.com/pdf/arttherapy-history.pdf

Canadian Art Therapy Association. (n.d.). Retrieved August 14, 2021, from Canadianarttherapy.org website: https://www.canadianarttherapy.org

(N.d.-b). Retrieved August 14, 2021, from http://https://www.concordia.
ca/academics/graduate/art-therapy.html#requirements

Entry requirements and training (art therapists/art psychotherapists).
(2015, April 30). Retrieved August 14, 2021, from Nhs.uk website:
https://www.healthcareers.nhs.uk/explore-roles/allied-health-
professionals/roles-allied-health-professions/art-therapistart-
psychotherapist/entry-requirements-and-training-art

What Kind of Therapy is Best for Me? (n.d.). Retrieved August 14,
2021, from Twochairs.com website: https://www.twochairs.com/blog/
what-kind-of-therapist-do-i-need

Raypole, C. (2019, March 1). Types of therapy: Different types of
approaches and how they work. Retrieved August 14, 2021, from
Healthline.com website: https://www.healthline.com/health/types-of-
therapy

Works Cited (Chapter 4)

Brown, A.D. Psychological benefits of art therapy. (2012). *Canadian
Counselling and Psychotherapy Association.* https://www.ccpa-accp.ca/
psychological-benefits-of-art-therapy/

Dresden, D. What is art therapy and how does it work. (2020).
Medical News Today. https://www.medicalnewstoday.com/articles/art-
therapy#how-it-works

Haeyen, S., Chakhssi, F., & Hooren, S.V. (2020). Benefits of
Art Therapy in People Diagnosed With Personality Disorders: A
Quantitative Survey. *Frontiers in Psychology.* https://doi.org/10.3389/
fpsyg.2020.00686

Nainis, N., Paice, J.A., Ratner, J., Wirth, J.H., Lai, J., & Shott, S.
(2006). Relieving Symptoms in Cancer: Innovative Use of Art Therapy.
Journal of Pain and Symptom Management, 31(2), 162-169. https://doi.
org/10.1016/j.jpainsymman.2005.07.006

Slayton, M.A., Sarah, C., D'Archer, J.M.A., & Kaplan, F.D.A. (2010. Outcome Studies on the Efficacy of Art Therapy: A Review of Findings. *Art Therapy, 27*(3), 108-118. https://doi.org/10.1080/07421656.2010.10 129660

Tiret, H. The benefits art therapy can have on mental and physical health. (2017). *Michigan State University.* https://www.canr.msu.edu/ news/the_benefits_art_therapy_can_have_on_mental_and_physical_ health

Upson, J. The role of art therapy in mental health and recovery. (2018). *Canadian Council on Rehabilitation and Work.* https://www.ccrw. org/2018/07/25/the-role-of- art-therapy-in-mental-health-recovery/

Works Cited (Chapter 5)

What is art therapy? — Canadian art therapy association [Internet]. Canadianarttherapy.org. [cited 2021 Jul 27]. Available from: https:// www.canadianarttherapy.org/what-is-art-therapy

Child art therapy: How it works. Psychology Today [Internet]. [cited 2021 Aug 9]; Available from: https://www.psychologytoday.com/ca/ blog/arts-and-health/201601/child-art-therapy-how-it-works

Benefits of expressive art therapy for children [Internet]. Georgetownbehavioral.com. [cited 2021 Aug 9]. Available from: https:// www.georgetownbehavioral.com/blog/expressive-art-therapy-for- children

Art therapy for seniors [Internet]. Completecare.ca. 2019 [cited 2021 Aug 9]. Available from: https://www.completecare.ca/blog/art-therapy- seniors/

ameriCARE. 8 benefits of art therapy for seniors [Internet]. Americareinfo.com. 2019 [cited 2021 Aug 9]. Available from: https:// www.americareinfo.com/8-benefits-of-art-therapy-for-seniors/

C-Care. The benefits of art therapy for seniors [Internet]. C-care.ca. 2017 [cited 2021 Aug 10]. Available from: https://www.c-care.ca/blog/elder-care/benefits-art-therapy-seniors/

Fabian R. How art therapy can heal PTSD [Internet]. Healthline.com. 2017 [cited 2021 Aug 10]. Available from: https://www.healthline.com/health/art-therapy-for-ptsd

Schouten KA MATh, van Hooren S PhD, Knipscheer JW PhD, Kleber RJ PhD, Hutschemaekers GJM PhD. Trauma-focused art therapy in the treatment of Posttraumatic Stress Disorder: A pilot study. J Trauma Dissociation. 2019;20(1):114–30.

Art therapy for post-traumatic stress disorder [Internet]. Mentalhealthcenter.org. 2020 [cited 2021 Aug 10]. Available from: https://www.mentalhealthcenter.org/art-therapy-for-post-traumatic-stress-disorder/

Klein Y. How art therapy will help with trauma [Internet]. Evolvetreatment.com. 2019 [cited 2021 Aug 10]. Available from: https://evolvetreatment.com/blog/art-therapy-trauma/

Forzoni S, Perez M, Martignetti A, Crispino S. Art therapy with cancer patients during chemotherapy sessions: an analysis of the patients' perception of helpfulness. Palliat Support Care. 2010;8(1):41–8.

Art therapy - Canadian cancer society [Internet]. Cancer.ca. [cited 2021 Aug 10]. Available from: https://www.cancer.ca/en/cancer-information/diagnosis-and-treatment/complementary-therapies/art-therapy/?region=on

Art therapy [Internet]. Cancerresearchuk.org. [cited 2021 Aug 10]. Available from: https://www.cancerresearchuk.org/about-cancer/cancer-in-general/treatment/complementary-alternative-therapies/individual-therapies/art-therapy

PEN Editorial Staff. Using art therapy to cope with cancer [Internet]. Powerfulpatients.org. 2019 [cited 2021 Aug 10]. Available from: https://powerfulpatients.org/2019/02/13/using-art-therapy-to-cope-with-cancer/

How art can help people understand and cope with depression – GeneSight [Internet]. Genesight.com. 2021 [cited 2021 Aug 10]. Available from: https://genesight.com/blog/patient/depression-art-help-understand-and-cope/

Kvarnstrom E. Using art therapy to create freedom from depression [Internet]. Bridgestorecovery.com. 2017 [cited 2021 Aug 10]. Available from: https://www.bridgestorecovery.com/blog/using-art-therapy-to-create-freedom-from-depression/

University of Gothenburg. Clear effect of art therapy on severe depression. Science Daily [Internet]. 2017 Nov 6 [cited 2021 Aug 10]; Available from: https://www.sciencedaily.com/releases/2017/11/171106100128.htm

Cassata C. Why art therapy may help you manage anxiety symptoms [Internet]. Psychcentral.com. 2021 [cited 2021 Aug 10]. Available from: https://psychcentral.com/anxiety/art-therapy-for-anxiety-relief

Tauber A. Does art therapy work for anxiety? Creativity and comprehensive treatment programs [Internet]. Bridgestorecovery.com. 2018 [cited 2021 Aug 10]. Available from: https://www.bridgestorecovery.com/blog/does-art-therapy-work-for-anxiety-creativity-and-comprehensive-treatment-programs/

Abbing A, Baars EW, de Sonneville L, Ponstein AS, Swaab H. The effectiveness of art therapy for anxiety in adult women: A randomized controlled trial. Front Psychol. 2019;10:1203.

Works Cited (Chapter 6)

Konopka LM. Where art meets neuroscience: a new horizon of art therapy. Croat Med J. 2014 Feb;55(1):73–4.

King JL, Kaimal G. Approaches to Research in Art Therapy Using Imaging Technologies. Front Hum Neurosci [Internet]. 2019 [cited 2021 Jul 20];0. Available from: https://www.frontiersin.org/articles/10.3389/fnhum.2019.00159/full

Bhattacharya J, Petsche H. Shadows of artistry: cortical synchrony during perception and imagery of visual art. Cogn Brain Res. 2002 Apr 1;13(2):179–86.

Cherry K. How Art Therapy Works [Internet]. Verywell Mind. 2021 [cited 2021 Jul 20]. Available from: https://www.verywellmind.com/what-is-art-therapy-2795755

Karkou V, Aithal S, Zubala A, Meekums B. Effectiveness of Dance Movement Therapy in the Treatment of Adults With Depression: A Systematic Review With Meta-Analyses. Front Psychol [Internet]. 2019 [cited 2021 Jul 27];0. Available from: https://www.frontiersin.org/articles/10.3389/fpsyg.2019.00936/full

Johnson DR. The theory and technique of transformations in drama therapy. Arts Psychother. 1991 Jan 1;18(4):285–300.

Klorer PG. Expressive Therapy with Severely Maltreated Children: Neuroscience Contributions. Art Ther. 2005 Jan;22(4):213–20.

Koelsch S. THE NEUROSCIENCES AND MUSIC III—DISORDERS AND PLASTICITY A Neuroscientific Perspective on Music Therapy. 2009.

Hopkins Medicine. Electroencephalogram (EEG) [Internet]. [cited 2021 Jul 28]. Available from: https://www.hopkinsmedicine.org/health/treatment-tests-and-therapies/electroencephalogram-eeg

Rauss K, Pourtois G. What is Bottom-Up and What is Top-Down in Predictive Coding? Front Psychol [Internet]. 2013 [cited 2021 Jul 28];0. Available from: https://www.frontiersin.org/articles/10.3389/fpsyg.2013.00276/full

Works Cited (Chapter 7)

Ball, B. (2002). Moments of change in the art therapy process. The Arts in Psychotherapy, 29(2), 79–92.

Bazargan, Y., and Pakdaman, S. (2016). The effectiveness of art therapy on reducing internalizing and externalizing problems of female adolescents. *Arch. Iran. Med.* 19, 51–56.

Bosgraaf, L., Spreen, M., Pattiselanno, K., & van Hooren, S. (2020). Art Therapy for Psychosocial Problems in Children and Adolescents: A Systematic Narrative Review on Art Therapeutic Means and Forms of Expression, Therapist Behavior, and Supposed Mechanisms of Change. *Frontiers in psychology, 11,* 584685. https://doi-org.myaccess.library.utoronto.ca/10.3389/fpsyg.2020.584685

Chandraiah S., Anand A. S., Avent L. C. (2012). Efficacy of group art therapy on depressive symptoms in adult heterogeneous psychiatric outpatients. *Art Ther.* 29, 80–86.

Crawford, M. J., Killaspy, H., Barnes, T. R., Barrett, B., Byford, S., Clayton, K., Dinsmore, J., Floyd, S., Hoadley, A., Johnson, T., Kalaitzaki, E., King, M., Leurent, B., Maratos, A., O'Neill, F. A., Osborn, D., Patterson, S., Soteriou, T., Tyrer, P., Waller, D., … MATISSE project team (2012). Group art therapy as an adjunctive treatment for people with schizophrenia: a randomised controlled trial (MATISSE). *Health technology assessment (Winchester, England)*, *16*(8), iii–76. https://doi-org.myaccess.library.utoronto.ca/10.3310/hta16080

Feldman M. B., Betts D. J., Blausey D. (2014). Process and outcome evaluation of an art therapy program for people living with HIV/AIDS. *Art Ther.* 31, 102–109

Kim S. K. (2013). A randomized, controlled study of the effects of art therapy on older Korean-Americans' healthy aging. *Arts Psychother.* 40, 158–164.

Leurent, B., Killaspy, H., Osborn, D. P., Crawford, M. J., Hoadley, A., Waller, D., & King, M. (2014). Moderating factors for the effectiveness of group art therapy for schizophrenia: secondary analysis of data from the MATISSE randomised controlled trial. *Social psychiatry and psychiatric epidemiology*, *49*(11), 1703–1710. https://doi-org.myaccess.library.utoronto.ca/10.1007/s00127-014-0876-2

Liu, C. (2017). *Examining the effectiveness of Solution-Focused Art Therapy (SF-AT) for sleep problems of children with traumatic experience.* Available online at: https://www.semanticscholar.org/paper/Examining-the-Effectiveness-of-Solution-Focused-Art-Liu/07047beab98ae0d76fad50d96ebc13f0da2d6ffb

Lyshak-Stelzer, F., Singer, P., St. John, P., & Chemtob, C. M. (2007). Art therapy for adolescents with posttraumatic stress disorder symptoms: A pilot study. Art Therapy: Journal of the American Art Therapy Association, 24(4), 163–169.

Matthew W. Reynolds PhD, Laura Nabors PhD & Anne Quinlan ATR (2000) The Effectiveness of Art Therapy: Does it Work?, Art Therapy, 17:3, 207-213. https://doi-org.myaccess.library.utoronto.ca/10.1080/074 21656.2000.10129706

Maujean, A., Pepping, C. A., & Kendall, E. (2014). A systematic review of randomized controlled studies of art therapy. *Art Therapy, 31*(1), 37–44. https://doi-org.myaccess.library.utoronto. ca/10.1080/07421656.2014.873696

McCaffrey, R., Liehr, P., Gregersen, T., & Nishioka, R. (2011). Garden walking and art therapy for depression in older adults: a pilot study. *Research in gerontological nursing, 4*(4), 237–242. https://doi-org. myaccess.library.utoronto.ca/10.3928/19404921-20110201-01

Monti, D. A., Kash, K. M., Kunkel, E. J., Brainard, G., Wintering, N., Moss, A. S., Rao, H., Zhu, S., & Newberg, A. B. (2012). Changes in cerebral blood flow and anxiety associated with an 8-week mindfulness programme in women with breast cancer. *Stress and health : journal of the International Society for the Investigation of Stress, 28*(5), 397–407. https://doi-org.myaccess.library.utoronto.ca/10.1002/smi.2470

Regev, D., & Cohen-Yatziv, L. (2018). Effectiveness of Art Therapy With Adult Clients in 2018-What Progress Has Been Made?. *Frontiers in psychology, 9*, 1531. https://doi-org.myaccess.library.utoronto. ca/10.3389/fpsyg.2018.01531

Reynolds, M. W., Nabors, L., & Quinlan, A. (2000). The effectiveness of art therapy: does it work?. *Art Therapy, 17*(3), 207-213.

Sela, N., Baruch, N., Assali, A., Vaturi, M., Battler, A., & Ben Gal, T. (2011). *Harefuah, 150*(2), 79–209.

Slayton, S.C., D'Archer, J., & Kaplan, F. (2010). Outcome Studies on the Efficacy of Art Therapy: A Review of Findings. *Art Therapy, 27*, 108 - 118. https://doi-org.myaccess.library.utoronto.ca/10.1080/07421656.20 10.10129660

Wikipedia contributors. (2021, February 12). American Art Therapy Association. In *Wikipedia, The Free Encyclopedia*. Retrieved 13:30, July 23, 2021, from https://en.wikipedia.org/w/index.php?title=American_ Art_Therapy_Association&oldid=1006443777